celebrating Guadalupe

celebrating Guadalupe

Jacqueline Orsini Dunnington

photographs by **Charles Mann**

RIO NUEVO PUBLISHERS

TUCSON, ARIZONA

RIO NUEVO PUBLISHERS
P.O. Box 5250, Tucson, Arizona 85703-0250
(520) 623-9558, www.rionuevo.com

Cover and interior design: Karen Schober, Seattle, Washington

The lines from *Labyrinth of Solitude* by Octavio Paz, © 1985, are reprinted by permission of Grove/Atlantic, Inc.

Front cover: painting by Gabe Vigil. • Back cover, clockwise from top: *The Arrival,* painting by Laura Brink;
custom boots by Rocket Buster Boots, El Paso, Texas; young celebrant in Mexico City. • Facing title page: Mexico City
street mural. • Contents page: sculpture by Rhonda Crespin.

Page 7: courtesy of the Museum of International Folk Art, Santa Fe, New Mexico (A.9.54-11B). • Page 11: courtesy of
Taylor Museum, Colorado Springs, Colorado. (TM 852) • Page 16: courtesy of Jorge G. Guadarrama, Museo de la Basílica
de Guadalupe, Basílica de Santa Maria de Guadalupe, Mexico. • Page 19 photo © 2003 by the Denver Art Museum. All
rights reserved. Funds contributed by Mr. and Mrs. George G. Anderman and an anonymous donor (1976.45). Published
version is cropped. • Page 60: courtesy of Skeleton Art Gallery, Santa Fe, New Mexico. • Page 67: boots courtesy of Lydia
Valdez, Back at the Ranch, Santa Fe, New Mexico. • Page 68: from the National Chicano Screenprint Taller, courtesy of
the Smithsonian American Art Museum (1991.65.3), a gift of the Wight Art Gallery, University of California, Los Angeles.

Library of Congress Cataloging-in-Publication Data

Dunnington, Jacqueline Orsini.
  Celebrating Guadalupe / Jacqueline Orsini Dunnington ; photographs by
Charles Mann.
     p. cm.
Includes bibliographical references.
  ISBN 1-887896-55-4
 1. Guadalupe, Our Lady of--Cult--New Mexico. 2. Guadalupe, Our Lady
of--Art. 3. Santos (Art)--New Mexico. 4. Folk art--New Mexico. 5. New
Mexico--Religious life and customs. I. Title.
  BT660.G82D86 2004
  232.91'7'097253--dc22
                              2003020755

Printed in Korea
10 9 8 7 6 5 4 3 2 1

contents

Framed
in flowers
and tinsel,
Guadalupe
appears in a
gift shop
window in
Ranchos de
Taos, New
Mexico.

CHAPTER ONE

She Is Everywhere

Celebrating Guadalupe is a tribute to the Virgin Mary as she has appeared in the New World. Almost from the moment of her first appearance in 1531, various groups and individuals have produced an abundance of images of Guadalupe, depicting her as comforter, healer, protector, agent of social justice, and symbol of Mexico itself. Depictions of Guadalupe in her various roles appear on everything from motorcycle decals to seventeenth-century religious paintings and every medium in between. For centuries, it has been chiefly through the eyes and hands of artisans—and through the many images of her that countless people have created—that we identify Our Lady of Guadalupe. To see her is to know her.

Guadalupe is widely celebrated in many public and private festivities, in countless artistic creations, and in ways that keep pace with the trends of the times. She has become a master symbol of the Mexican and

La Santísima Virgen de Guadalupe, a traditional painted wood figure by José Rafael Aragón, early nineteenth century.

Devotional painting by a Salvadoran artist named Crucita, 2002.

Mexican-American people, and her popularity is spreading to other cultural groups as well. The miraculous story of her appearances on Tepeyac Hill (near what is now Mexico City) has transcended language barriers and cultural differences. Cities, mountains, and rivers now bear her name, as do people, shrines, and even commercial products.

In time, depictions of the Mexican Guadalupe traveled to all continents and into millions of lives. In the United States alone, more than three hundred churches, institutions, and societies are dedicated to her. Abroad, her likeness appears so widely that she easily could be called "Global Guadalupe." Copies of the original image that appeared on Juan Diego's cloak, or *tilma,* hang in the Cathedral of Nôtre Dame in Paris; in the cathedral in Addis Ababa, Ethiopia; and inside the Church of the Infant of Prague in the Czech Republic. In Italy her portrait graces a wall in the Church of San Stefano at Aveto and dominates a chapel dedicated to her at the Shrine of the Holy House at Loreto. Guadalupe is visually present in multiple locations in Rome: at a church atop Monte Mario, in the Vatican garden, at a church dedicated to her on the Via Aurelia, and in a shrine deep under St. Peter's Basilica dedicated to her in 1992. Guadalupe's portraits, both pious and daring, also appear in Asian sites such as Kyoto, Japan; Pondicherry, India; and throughout the Philippines.

Fiddlers
Ken Keppeler
and Jeanie
McLerie,
Silver City,
New Mexico.

CHAPTER TWO

The 1531 Legend

The traditional story, usually told in four parts, opens before sunrise on December 9, 1531, as Juan Diego, a Christianized Nahua (more commonly referred to as an Aztec), was hastening to Mass. His native name was Quauhtlatoatzin ("The Eagle Speaks"). He took a route that led him to a place on the northeast rim of Mexico City (then called Tenochtitlán in the local language, Nahuatl).

As Juan Diego reached Tepeyac (or Tepeyacac in Nahuatl) Hill on a Saturday morning, music "like the songs of various precious birds" filled the air. He paused to listen, but soon the birds fell silent. Then a woman called out to him from the hilltop, saying, "Dear Juan, dear Juan Diego." The tale continues with his vision of a lady whose garments were "like the sun in the way they gleamed and shone." The rocks on the hill glistened, and the cactus seemed very green with golden thorns. She spoke and asked him where he was going; he answered that he was "pursuing the divine matters"—that is, he

Our Lady of Guadalupe, by the Truchas Master, early nineteenth century.

Painting by
Alexandra Starr
Damron y
Valdez, Youth
Award winner,
Santa Fe
Spanish
Colonial Arts
Society Winter
Market, 2001.
(photo by
Gene Peach)

was going to Mass. The woman then intro-duced herself as the "the eternal consum-mate virgin Saint Mary, mother of the very true deity, God," and requested that a tem-ple be built for her where she was standing. Supposedly this was the

site of a shrine once consecrated to a local goddess of fertility, rain, and lunar cycles, usually identified as Tonantzin. However, some scholars question the importance and even the validity of Tonantzin's connection to the spot where this Virgin Mary first stood on Mexican soil. The name "Tonantzin" could have identified several female deities—or perhaps one collective earth goddess, who possessed attributes both as creators and destroyers of all life. To most devout Christians, however, Mary (and hence Guadalupe) represents a triumph over such pagan archetypes.

According to a version of the story writ-ten in 1649, she further assured Juan Diego of her will "to give to people all my love, aid, and protection." This wish was for the "various people who love me, who cry out to me, who seek me, who trust me." The Virgin requested that Juan Diego go to the bishop and ask that he build a "temple" for her. The Nahua fell to his knees, then went

La Madre Tonantsin, a thirty-two-foot mural near
Castro Street in San Francisco, by Colette Crutcher.
Guadalupe appears as the goddess' third eye.

directly to see the Spanish-born bishop-elect of Mexico, Don Fray Juan de Zumárraga, to whom he related this wondrous encounter through an interpreter. However, the bishop-elect doubted the humble Juan Diego's report, and Juan's initial ardor was dampened by this rejection.

Later the same day Juan Diego returned to Tepeyac Hill "grieving" over his failed mission. He then begged the heavenly Lady to find a more important person to deliver her request, "one of the high nobles" and

not "a poor ordinary man" such as himself. During this second apparition, she did not accept his plea of being a man too unimportant for the task. The lady urged him to return the next day, Sunday, to see the bishop-elect again. "And be sure to tell him again how it is really myself, the Ever Virgin Saint Mary, the Mother of God the deity, who is sending you there."

That Sunday, Juan Diego once again hastened to the bishop-elect's palace, waited for hours, and finally was able to enter a second plea on behalf of the "heavenly lady." This time, Zumárraga asked that the humble native provide proof of the woman's identity. After this meeting, the bishop-elect ordered some of his staff to follow Juan Diego and check on his activities, but the scouts were unable to find Juan Diego and returned to Zumárraga vexed over their wasted time.

Monday, Juan Diego did not return to Tepeyac, for he kept vigil at the bedside of

This pillow unites the Virgin with the Stars and Stripes.

Young boy
dressed as
Juan Diego
in front of a
mural at the
basilica in
Mexico City.

Detail from
the original
tilma image.

his dying uncle, Juan Bernadino. The old man, suffering from an illness presumed to be fatal, asked the Nahua to summon a priest for last rites of the church.

Before sunrise the following day, Tuesday, Juan Diego set off to fulfill his uncle's final plea. He attempted to avoid the "Ever Virgin" because of his uncle's imminent death. However, she intercepted him en route at the eastern edge of Tepeyac and inquired, "Where are you going?" He answered that he was going to summon a priest for his dying uncle. The "compassionate, consummate Virgin" assured Juan Diego that his uncle had already recovered. The "heavenly lady," as intercessor, had thus performed her first healing on Mexican soil, launching a tradition of therapeutic miracles linked to *Nuestra Señora* (Our Lady) *de Guadalupe,* as she would eventually be called. The Virgin assured Juan Diego that she would now prove her true identity. He was directed to return to the spot where they had first met, at the hilltop, where he would see "various kinds of flowers growing."

The Virgin assisted Juan Diego in gathering the flowers as she "took them in her arms" and wrapped the blossoms in the fold of his tilma—a rustic cloak most likely woven from the maguey agave plant, *ayotl.* She instructed him to take the blossoms to the bishop-elect as final proof of her identity, and thus he should honor her request for a temple. The conclusion of the fourth apparition has the Nahua revisiting Zumárraga, this time with a sure sign that "the heavenly Lady, St. Mary" had unquestionably appeared. When Juan Diego unfolded his cloak, "fine flowers in the Spanish style" fell to the ground at Zumárraga's feet, and the famous "miraculous portrait" featuring "the precious image of the consummate Virgin Saint Mary, mother of God the deity, was imprinted and appeared on the cloak." This legend became a central part of Mexican heritage.

How the Story Spread

In 1648 a priest named Miguel Sánchez (1594–1674) published a landmark Spanish-language version of the December 1531 story, 117 years after the reputed apparitions. This account is the first major written text of the entire story. Sánchez relied heavily on oral history provided by people he trusted. He also linked the apparitions to numerous events and people in the Bible.

In 1649, Luis Laso (also spelled Lasso or Lazo) de la Vega published an account in Nahuatl of the Virgin of Guadalupe's apparitions, called the *Nican Mopohua.* His account is said to be partially based on an early, now lost, document titled *Relación,* attributed to a Nahua—Antonio Valeriano (d. 1605)—who had mastered Latin. Scholars are not sure whether this early document ever existed, or if so, the depth of its influence on the 1649 text. The *Nican Mopohua* was primarily intended for a native Mesoamerican audience.

Certainly oral accounts and perhaps some now-lost, handwritten versions of the apparition story had circulated throughout central Mexico before these two texts appeared, and Guadalupe as a visual icon and a devotional cult had already started to blossom. However, the 1648 and 1649 publications marked a permanent change in New World devotion to Guadalupe. After this, the written word supplemented spoken stories and undeniably helped her massive spread to all sectors

Sculpture by Eulogio and Zoraida Ortega, Velarde, New Mexico.

Our Lady of Guadalupe, 1779, oil painting by Sebastián Salcedo of Mexico.

of Mexico and beyond. These documents would mark a new era in Guadalupe's importance and eventually help lead to her status as Mexico's premier symbol.

These two publications, though they varied considerably in style and coverage of the apparition story, quite possibly recorded the story of Guadalupe and Juan Diego for the first time in printed form. The text of the *Nican Mopohua* became the basic account of the apparitions.

The Story Is Retold in Pictures

Even today, Guadalupe is best known through visual images, presented to us through the eyes and hands of artists. She has become a highly familiar vessel of belief, commemorated in the arts, souvenirs, Christian rituals, family tributes, names of places and of people, public ceremonies, papal favor, and lore.

Many devotees of Guadalupe truly believe that a divine agent created the image in the "miraculous portrait." In the tranlslated words of the 1649 *Nican Mopohua:* "It was by divine miracle that she appeared…absolutely no earthly person had painted her precious image." Several famous paintings from the Spanish Colonial period even show God's divine paintbrush as he creates this visual miracle.

However, for nearly five hundred years, sermons, scholars, and scientists have challenged the miraculous origin of the Virgin of Guadalupe's seminal portrait. One puzzling factor is that Zumárraga, an educated and highly literate clergyman, does not mention the December 1531 apparitions or related events in either his memoirs or his will. This is just one instance of the blocks in the quest for the truth. The deeper one digs into the story, the more confusing the diverse data (or lack of data) may become, for those who require logical explanations.

Diversity is also an important aspect of a larger pattern—the seemingly limitless

VENERATION OF THE TILMA

The tilma image has been sheltered in five structures over the centuries. The first is said to have been an adobe chapel near Tepeyac Hill. The second, called the Hermitage of Montúfar and constructed of stone and mortar— possibly on the same spot as the original structure—was dedicated in 1556. The third building, built of solid masonry at the base of Tepeyac Hill, was started in 1609 and dedicated in 1622. The fourth structure was finished in 1709 on the same site as the third; it was the first one to be declared a basilica—an official designation given by the Vatican based on historical, artistic, and pastoral requirements. It suffered damage from sinking foundations, and although it still stands, it is closed to the public. The nearby fifth edifice, the Basílica de Nuestra Señora de Guadalupe, opened in 1976 and has become the most visited pilgrimage site in the Western Hemisphere, second only to the Vatican worldwide. Its modern design is engineered to withstand the underground tremors typical of the area. Any basilica dedicated to Mary has roots in antiquity. One of the oldest church buildings in Christendom dedicated to the Virgin Mary, La Basilica di Santa Maria in Trastevere in Rome, rests on a foundation laid in A.D. 217.

Late-
nineteenth-
century
painting by a
Tarahumara
Indian artist.
(photo by
Jacqueline
Dunnington)

renderings of both Guadalupe and Juan Diego in the visual arts. For example, although roses have become the commonly accepted flowers in the story, other terms abounded in both written and oral accounts—such as "precious Spanish flowers," "flowers of Castile," or lilies, violets, and jasmine. If indeed the actual blossoms of the apparition were Spanish or from Castile, the plant is probably the *Rosa foetida* bicolor—a small five-petal rose still popular in the American Southwest and Mexico. No flowers of any species appear on the original tilma image.

Artists would eventually favor hybrid roses in the Guadalupan visual arts, both in whimsical and botanically accurate examples. New floral species have also bloomed in the artistic traditions of Spanish Colonial, folk, and pop art interpretations of Guadalupe, but roses have developed into the dominant visual metaphor for the blooming of Guadalupe as she was celebrated in Mexico and elsewhere.

A pilgrim's staff, or *quiote,* near Las Cruces, New Mexico.

CHAPTER THREE

The San Juan Diego Story

Pope John Paul II elevated Juan Diego to sainthood in the Roman Catholic Church on July 31, 2002, at the Basílica de Guadalupe in Mexico City, making him the first indigenous person from what is now Mexico to receive this honor. December 9 will be San Juan Diego's official feast day, in remembrance of the date generally regarded as Guadalupe's first appearance to him.

Juan Diego was officially beatified on July 6, 1990, and known for twelve years thereafter as Blessed Juan Diego. This status meant that he was worthy of public and private veneration. The final piece of the required data to qualify him for beatitude arose, in part, from an incident that took place in Mexico City. According to several accounts, in May of 1990 a young man, upset or on drugs, fell or flung himself from a building and smashed his skull during an apparent attempt at suicide. His mother, Señora Silva—a devout believer—immediately asked Juan Diego for

A man portrays Juan Diego in East Los
Angeles, California.

In front of the old basilica, dancers honor
Guadalupe on December 12.

an intercession to God via Guadalupe on behalf of her stricken son. The young man was reportedly taken to a hospital, where the medical staff declared the case hopeless. Yet a few days later, the injured man returned to life. Juan Diego's plea on behalf of the man's mother is given popular credit for his survival.

This miracle story is highly reminiscent of similar tales harking back to early cures associated with the 1531 events. Juan Diego's uncle, Juan Bernadino, enjoyed remission from a life-threatening illness after Guadalupe appeared. Legend also has it that on December 26, 1531—the feast of the first Christian martyr, St. Stephen—an arrow struck the body of a Mesoamerican in a procession commemorating the Virgin's recent manifestations. This victim, reputed to have been temporarily dead, is said to have survived because Guadalupe interceded on his behalf and asked God to save him. This restorative act was taken as proof

positive of her promise to Juan Diego to help his people. Soon, reports about this second medical miracle circulated throughout the region. The power of folk devotion, in the absence of modern medicine, has given Guadalupe's vow to Juan Diego direct credit for working therapeutic wonders.

The history of sainthood is long and complex. According to the New Testament, even a living Christian can be a saint, although official sainthood has always been granted posthumously. Apostles, confessors, evangelists, martyrs, and those who lead austere lives in the cause of spiritual purity can be proclaimed as saints if they perform miracles. Eighty-one of the 263 popes dating from St. Peter to John Paul II have been named saints, although only three have achieved this honor in the past nine hundred years. Juan Diego, on the other hand, never joined a religious order.

After Bishop Ulric of Augsburg was declared a saint in A.D. 993, papal canonization became necessary to reach sainthood beyond local recognition. Once declared, a saint belongs to the whole church. Saints are never worshiped, but those who ask help from God may often implore a saint, or saints, to intercede for them. Trades, professions, and people with various maladies are protected by specific saints. San Juan Diego is now the patron saint and protector of the indigenous peoples and the Model for the Lay Apostolate.

What Is Known of Juan Diego's Life and His Appearance

There is no known text dating from the era of the apparition legend containing absolutely certified information about Juan Diego. His biography, taken from oral and written sources, offers contradictions and puzzles. Because the details of Juan Diego's life, like the Guadalupe story, combine bits of folklore with conflicting data and historical views, we will probably neverknow the true story.

Carlos de Sigüenza y Góngora, in 1689, said that Juan Diego was born about the year 1474. He was the first to give Juan Diego a native name (Quauhtlatoatzin, "The Eagle Speaks"). In this account, the Nahua was baptized with his wife, María Lucía, in 1524, and thereafter they lived in celibacy until her death prior to the apparitions. He was said to be fifty-seven in 1531. Other biographical sketches of Juan Diego appear in muddled records, the similar so-called "wills" of Juana Martín, perhaps a relative of Juan Diego, and Gregoria María. The latter states that Juan Diego's wife was named Malintzin

Mural enhances a video store in Tucson, Arizona.

(not María Lucía) and that she died soon after their marriage. This document also implies that he was a young man at the time of the apparitions (not fifty-seven) and that his wife died a few days before they occurred. A third summary of Juan Diego's life was presented in 1666 by Luis Becerra Tanco, who claimed that Juan Diego's wife died two years after the apparitions. In the 1785 *Estrella del Norte de México,* Francisco de Florencia, S.J., suggested that Juan Diego's wife died in 1529 and that he had a son, possibly by an earlier wife, or perhaps a child that he adopted.

Artists present many different images of Juan Diego. Nobody knows for certain what his physical appearance was; the first paintings depicting him did not appear until the seventeenth century, long after his death. As time went on, Juan Diego's role in the Guadalupe legend was portrayed in a multitude of ways. He is often featured in the presence of Bishop Zumárraga, either kneeling or standing, as he displays his tilma. Other formats include inserts depicting the four appearances of the Virgin to Juan Diego. He is also rendered standing as he holds, or wears, the tilma bearing Guadalupe's portrait.

The convention of giving him a beard or facial hair contradicts the fact that native Nahuas bore little or no facial hair. All major pre-Columbian illustrated manuscripts (called codices) reflect this. Yet some portraits of Juan Diego display a flowing beard on his face, others a modest mustache, sometimes with a goatee. His portrayals in the visual arts also offer a veritable catalog of male hair styles that range from a tumble of dark locks to a bald head with just a skimpy fringe of hair. Juan Diego's appearance—body type, hair, skin tones, and clothing—is totally derived from imagination and lore, not from biological fact or from a portrait made in his lifetime.

Visual artists have shown his garments in equally inconsistent ways, many of them

next page: Pilgrims gather at the modern basilica in Mexico City. Old basilica stands on the right.

completely unrelated to the styles of cloth-ing the native people wore around the time of the arrival of the Spaniards. In some instances Juan Diego is dressed in baggy trousers; in others, his legs are bare; and in others, he may wear a simple tunic, varying from long to short. Some painters dress the new saint in a bland mix of monastic garb not associated with any specific order. When he wears a tilma over his shoulders and tied to the side or front, Juan Diego's clothing approximates the true style of his era.

Juan Diego's portraits show a wide array of head coverings—from a straw sombrero dangling upon his shoulders to a head scarf worn in a near-Muslim manner—or some-times he is shown bareheaded. Even if the Nahuas of that era wore either simple or elaborate headdresses, these were still not the hats that men of today or the past half millennium have known. As for his feet, Juan Diego generally wears sandals or appears barefooted.

One of the most touching ways to memorialize him is to dress a young boy as Juan Diego for events celebrating Guada-lupe, especially on her feast day of Decem-ber 12. Scores of these young, human representations wear mustaches painted on their faces in memory of Juan Diego's popu-lar presentations. The boy usually carries a gourd filled with water and bears a charm-ing token—a tiny birdcage—echoing the story line that birds warbled to Juan Diego of the Virgin's arrival in December 1531.

Trinkets and souvenirs reflecting Juan Diego's role in the Guadalupe story have been sparse in comparison with those of the Virgin. Mass-produced pictures of the saint, standing alone and holding a reproduction of his imprinted tilma, are primarily found on votive candles, plastic prayer cards, medallions, key rings, and other amulets. Early in 2002, following the canonization announcement from the Vatican in 2001, T-shirts with the saint's image—many of them

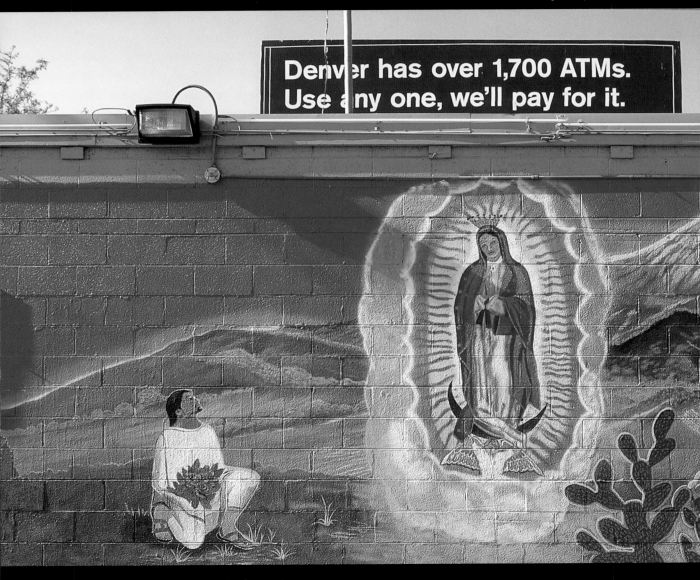

Grocery store wall in Denver, Colorado.

Young
celebrant in
Mexico
City.

manufactured in Asia—flooded the *mercados* (markets) adjacent to the basilica in Mexico City. By Easter Sunday 2002 and the canonization date later that summer, hats, scarves, and other items of clothing featuring Juan Diego were for sale in abundance throughout Mexico City.

His Name and Other Persisting Questions

The newly canonized saint's name is another interesting topic. The name Juan, along with that of Guadalupe, came into vogue during the late eighteenth century in Mexico. He has also been dubbed "Juan Dieguito."

Numerous associations, be they from the pulpit, printed matter, or personal opinions, link Juan Diego's role in the apparition sequence with prominent biblical figures. He has been called the "Moses of Mexico." In this interpretation, Tepeyac is the new Zion or Sinai. Juan Diego is also frequently called the "Santiago of Mexico," likening him to the Spanish pilgrim and martyr St. James, who brought Christianity to the pagans of northern Spain and Portugal. Such links to religious legends of the Old World gave Mexico the aura of a promised land.

A stunning theory about the image on Juan Diego's tilma was put forth in a 1794 sermon delivered in Mexico City by a Dominican, Fray Servando Teresa de Mier. He claimed that the image of the Virgin dates from long before 1531—indeed, that it came into form on the cloak of St. Thomas when he met with the Virgin in Mexico. Mier believed that the apostle visited Mexico several centuries prior to Guadalupe's apparitions—and in fact prior to the arrival of the Europeans in the New World. Mier's notion would thus place the tilma image's divine origin shortly after the death of Christ. There is no other source for this opinion; the cloak of St. Thomas has never been found either in the Americas or at Mt. Saint Thomas in Mylapore, India, where the apostle is said to have traveled and where his bones may be buried.

Many questions about Juan Diego persist. Some ask, did he really exist? What was his role in his community? What were his physical attributes? Was he a divinely selected man, or an accidental participant in the apparition sequence? The scholar D. A. Brading concluded that there may well have been a Nahua Indian named Juan living close to Tepeyac at some point in the sixteenth century. However, suppositions about Juan Diego are just hypothetical, since there is no reliable, surviving written evidence. The significance of San Juan Diego, as with Guadalupe, is that the known factual data about him are overshadowed by the vitality of his presence in Mexican popular culture.

THE MIRACULOUS SPRING AT TEPEYAC HILL

Another marvel exists in the area where the apparitions occurred, which enabled the European Christians to further share their heritage of miracles with the Mesoamerican people. At Tepeyac, a natural spring flows at the very spot where Juan Diego is said to have gathered flowers. These waters were, and still are, reputed to bring about medical cures to those who drink and bathe in them. The spring waters that flow downward deepen into a well that was rerouted in 1776 to an open, stone-walled basin; in 1777, construction of the El Pocito Chapel was begun at the site of the well, and you can still visit this chapel today, a short distance away from the basilica.

In honor of
Juan Diego's
native roots,
traditional
Aztec
costumes
enliven
Mexico
City on
December 12.

CHAPTER FOUR

Guadalupe's History and the Miraculous Portrait

The story of the New World Guadalupe is not a closed book—in fact, her legend and her cult are still developing. She is not the simple product of a gentle commingling of European and Mesoamerican religious heritage. Yet these combined traditions, along with political and historic events, eventually led to the formation of a world-famous Marian icon. Today sites about Guadalupe and San Juan Diego abound on the Internet. Her presence as a symbol is commemorated in the arts and in rituals, communal festivities, and accounts both oral and written. For her followers she is intangible and ineffable—a link between the human and the divine.

Millions of people in the Americas celebrate Guadalupe as the Virgin Mary at the opening of the twenty-first century. In the United States, we can find a concentration of her importance in the states that border Mexico: Texas, New Mexico, Arizona, and California—although her influence

Tapestry of the Virgin, Cathedral Santuario de Guadalupe (also called Cathedral Guadalupe), Dallas, Texas. (photo by Buzzy Drews)

The original tilma hangs high on the wall inside the Mexico City basilica.

Guadalupe
T-shirts for
sale near the
basilica.

stretches far beyond this area as well. Her followers dance in front of her image, they sing to her, they bow their heads in front of her likeness. Her devotees pray to her to intercede for their most pressing needs. The Mother of the Americas is not a passive icon sheltered in a religious structure; she is invoked for benedictions outside church walls, in active contact with her people.

Newspapers give ample coverage to visions of Guadalupe appearing on such diverse surfaces as cloth blinds in New Mexico, a yucca plant in Arizona, a puddle of melted ice cream in a Houston, Texas,

Traditional *matachín* headdresses at the annual Guadalupe celebration in Tortugas, New Mexico.

building complex, and a tile in the Hidalgo stop in the Mexico City subway system. (This tile is now protected in a small glass-covered shelter in front of which devotees leave coins as they utter quiet prayers.)

Guadalupe's Story Spreads Northward

Guadalupe entered what is now the United States when much of the American Southwest was still part of New Spain. She first reached the Rio Grande at the present border crossing between El Paso, Texas, and Ciudad Juárez, Mexico. Fray García de San Francisco, O.F.M., is often credited with founding the Misión de Nuestra Señora de Guadalupe de los Mansos del Paso del Norte on the Juárez side of the river, possibly in 1659, and Guadalupe's story soon spread to the other side as well.

A large shrine in Port Arthur, Texas.

In 1663, Fray Juan Ramírez wrote of his travels to Socorro, in the state now called New Mexico, accompanied by an image of Nuestra Señora de Guadalupe. In 1680 the famous Pueblo Revolt took place in the northern part of the state, and the non-natives fled south for safety and settled the towns of Ysleta, Socorro, and San Elizario, where they too met the cult of Guadalupe. (El Paso was also settled in 1680, but not incorporated as a town until 1873.)

Devotion to Guadalupe moved northward and bloomed after the peaceful 1692 return of the exiled residents to the upper Rio Grande corridor. The oldest still-standing church dedicated to Guadalupe in the United States is in Santa Fe, New Mexico, at the end of the old Camino Real. A license to perform sacraments at the *capilla* (chapel) was granted in October 1795; the Santuario

On Guadalupe's feast day, dancers celebrate in the streets of Chihuahua City, Mexico.

A statue of Juan Diego in Juárez, Mexico, seems to glow with the appearance of Guadalupe. (photo by Jacqueline Dunnington)

de Guadalupe now falls under the direction of the Guadalupe Historic Foundation. In 1699 a Christian mission church at Zuni Pueblo was dedicated to Guadalupe, and although its name and dedication changed several times after that (and various church buildings have come and gone over the years), the site itself was rededicated to Guadalupe in 1754. More periods of abandonment and reactivation have followed.

Father Eusebio Francisco Kino, S.J. (1645–1711), a Jesuit born in the Tyrolean Alps (in what is now part of Italy), was devoted to another Guadalupe—the dark Virgin of Guadalupe from Cáceres, Spain (this Spanish Guadalupe had become the divine patroness of navigators, including Columbus, by the 1400s). In 1683 Kino journeyed to Baja California and established the Misión de Nuestra Señora de Guadalupe in the coastal community now called La Paz. Later, he traveled north through what would become the Mexican state of Sonora and southern Arizona, where he likely introduced his Guadalupe—who by now surely embodied both Old World and New World traditions—to tribal groups he met. Missionary work in the northern Sonoran Desert since Kino's era has endorsed devotion to the New World Guadalupe, and today she is a highly visible presence in Arizona. In fact, the town of Guadalupe, which lies within the Greater Phoenix metropolitan area, was founded and so named in the early 1900s by Yaqui Indians seeking refuge from persecution by the Mexican government of Porfirio Díaz.

Guadalupe's entry into the state of California came after Blessed Junípero Serra founded the first of California's twenty-one missions, San Diego de Alcalá, in 1769. Although we find no specific records of any devotion to Guadalupe at that time, images of her soon appeared in many of the mission churches. In 1845, Bishop Diego García established the first college in the state at

Santa Inés and dedicated it to Guadalupe. For the past century, Guadalupe has enjoyed wide popularity among California's farm workers and city dwellers alike, from the barrios to the art studios. Pastoral endorsement has furthered the veneration of La Madrecita, and on the Feast of Guadalupe in December, streets in East Los Angeles explode with crowded celebrations.

The Spanish Guadalupe

The visual differences between the Mexican and Spanish Guadalupes are striking, but there is one telling link between the two: They share the same name. The name Guadalupe may have been brought to Mexico after 1519 by Cortés (who was born not far from the Cáceres monastery), his troops, or other Spaniards. The New World Virgin Mary of Guadalupe has been known by this Spanish-origin name since the earliest mention of her 1531 apparitions.

This has also been the name of a large monastery in Cáceres, in the Extremadura region of western Spain, built during the 1300s. A small wooden statue of the Spanish Guadalupe is on display inside this Spanish monastery. The diminutive statue was carved from dark wood with an extra layer of dark paint, and a small, equally dark Jesus sits on her left arm. Another carving of the Virgin Mary resides inside this monastery. In this low-relief image, high above the monastery floor, Mary is encircled by a body halo of sun rays as she stands above a sliver of the moon. Some scholars wonder if the tilma portrait could have been indirectly inspired by this example, as well as by the general reservoir of Spanish art circulating in Mexico after the conquest.

The Church Embraces Guadalupe

On April 24, 1754, Pope Benedict XIV bestowed the honor of the Mass and Office

This mural transforms a wooden fence in Taos
County, New Mexico.

A young woman rides in the back of a pickup truck in a two-mile-long procession in East Los Angeles.

(the doctrinal words) for Our Lady of Guadalupe. A month later, he not only established her official feast day as December 12 (the day of her final appearance to San Juan Diego), but he also made a famous statement, saying of God that "He has not dealt thus with all nations" (in Latin, *Non fecit taliter omni nationi*), adapted from Psalm 147.

By the 1550s, a chapel dedicated to Guadalupe stood at the Tepeyac site. After the legend began to have limited circulation around the greater Mexico City area, but not yet deeply into the far reaches of the nation, anti-apparitionist voices were heard. In 1556, a Franciscan, Francisco de Bustamante, delivered a sermon attacking the nascent devotional cult, which he condemned as a mixture of pagan and native goddess worship at Tepeyac. There has been a continuum of skeptical voices denouncing the legend since the late 1500s. In 1996, Guillermo Schulenburg, abbot of the Mexican Basílica de Guadalupe, challenged the entire Guadalupan story in well-publicized statements. He was forced to resign his post.

Endorsement from the Vatican and other high posts helped to spread Guadalupe's influence across the Americas. In 1910, Pope Pius X decreed that the

An enthusiastic marcher in the same parade.

image of Guadalupe was the "Glory and Refuge of the Latin American Nations." Pope Pius XII named her Empress of the Americas in 1945. In 1979 Pope John Paul II presented a silver- and gold-plated tiara to Guadalupe during the first papal visit in history to the Western Hemisphere. On July 31, 2002, Mexico's president Vicente Fox, a devotee of Guadalupe, joined more than twenty thousand fellow worshippers gathered inside the Basílica de Guadalupe for the canonization ceremony of San Juan Diego, celebrated by Pope John Paul II during his fourth visit to Mexico.

Changes in Her Image over Time

Just as various sources present divergent views of Guadalupe's legend, these differences become even more noticeable in the visual arts. In fact, even the original portrait on Juan Diego's cloak has been altered over the years.

The tilma bearing the original image of the Virgin of Guadalupe—the "miraculous portrait," as it is often called—now hangs in the Basilica of Guadalupe in Mexico City. Several decades after this imprint of the Virgin is said to have appeared on the tilma, unknown artisans started to alter it. These alterations contributed not only depth but ambiguities to the Guadalupe story. Some believe the insertions reflect biblical and European traditions, while others relate most of the added symbols to Mesoamerican iconography.

The portrait on Juan Diego's cloak embodies a complex fusion of religious symbols: a body halo, a sliver of the moon, an angel, a cherub or cherubs, and stars on the Virgin's mantle. However, the original portrait of Guadalupe included only her face and her body to just below the knees. Her hands are clasped in prayer, and she wears a soft greenish-blue mantle and pink underdress. The materials used to depict

these original elements remain unidentifiable, with no visible brush strokes on original portions of the image on the tilma and certain pigments that do not respond to infrared detection. Some scientists believe that these details can be explained; after all, Mesoamerican artisans painted with feathers that leave no stroke marks, and certain pigments used in the sixteenth century, such as azurite, actually absorb infrared light and prevent examination of underlying layers. One study, approved by the Catholic Church and using infrared examination, revealed that all the black and gold details, including the angel, the moon, the waistband, and the neck pendant, were obviously later human additions, as was the elongation of her body. Over time, numerous sources have claimed that a certain Marcos de Aquino Cipac created Guadalupe's basic portrait; such opinions draw upon a reference in an official 1556 investigation of this matter.

Some people who have seen photographs of Guadalupe's miracle portrait are convinced that they detect a microscopic configuration of a man's face on the front rim of the Virgin's right eye, although the church-endorsed study indicates that all the black paint was added to the original image by human hands. Some people claim this is a portrait of San Juan Diego, although the figure does sport a beard, which was not traditional for Nahua men of that time.

Traditional Meanings of the Added Symbols

Traditional European elements added to the basic composition of the "miraculous portrait" include the sun, crown, body halo, moon, and an angel at Guadalupe's feet. Such details had been common in the Christian arts of Europe prior to 1531 and reflect two different ways of looking at Mary. The first way features Mary as the

Virgin of the Immaculate Conception, "all beautiful," without the baby Jesus on her left arm. The Immaculate Conception doctrine arose after 1128, though it had early roots in eastern Christianity. It was proclaimed dogma by the Vatican in 1854.

The second concept derives from the Woman of the Apocalypse described in

Guadalupe's image decorates everything from air freshener and hot sauce to hats and wallets.

Revelation 12:1: "A great sign appeared in the sky, a woman clothed with the sun, with the moon under her feet, and on her head a crown of twelve stars." These symbols are highly relevant to Marian art in general, and in particular to Guadalupe. The reference to

A ROSE BY ANY OTHER NAME

Guadalupe's diverse names reflect the highly personal presence she occupies among the millions of her ardent followers. Her many names include:

The Brown Virgin

Coatlaxopeuh (a speculative Nahuatl-based name meaning "the one who crushed the serpent's head")

La Criolla

The Dark Virgin

Emperatriz de América

Empress of the Americas

Madonna of the Barrios

Madre Guadalupe, La Madrecita

La Morena, La Morenita

Mother of the Americas, Mother of the People

Nuestra Señora, Nuestra Señora de Guadalupe

Our Lady of Guadalupe, Our Lady

Our Queen

La Pastora

Queen of the Americas

Reina de América

Reina de México

Tequanatlanopeuh (a speculative Nahuatl-based name meaning "she who originates from the rocks")

Tlecuauhtlapcupeuh (a speculative Nahuatl-based name meaning "she who emerges from the region of light like the eagle from fire")

La Virgen, La Virgencita

La Virgen de Guadalupe

La Virgen de Tepeyac

The Virgin Mary of Guadalupe

The Virgin of Guadalupe

The Virgin of Tepeyac

being clothed by the sun is of extreme importance for Guadalupe, who eclipsed sun worship in Mesoamerica to become "a great sign" bridging Europe and the New World.

Guadalupe was also seen as the one who blocked the pagan sun god. In 1652, a Mercedarian, Diego Rodríguez, claimed that a comet of the same year, along with eclipses that shaded the sun, were auspicious omens indicating that Guadalupe would bring wisdom to Mexico.

While most art historians see the combination of the body halo, crescent moon, and crown as reflections of European Christian views, others prefer a Mesoamerican basis for these symbols. They take the Virgin as blocking the rays of the Aztec god of sun and war, and the lunar sliver to be a native female symbol.

A crown for Guadalupe's head was added to the original portrait—most likely in the late 1500s—then removed in the late 1880s. In Christian art, the artist may place a crown as an article of honor, victory, or royalty upon the head of a martyr, pope, or saint, although the crowning of sacred images did not become an official Vatican procedure until 1837. In 1895, Pope Leo XIII held an official, Vatican-sanctioned coronation ritual for Guadalupe. She remains the popular Queen of the Americas with or without this royal symbol. (One interesting note: We find no known golden crowns atop the heads of pre-Columbian goddesses.)

By the middle of the seventeenth century, artisans were often inspired to add more details to Guadalupan portraits. In general, these additions illustrated the 1531 legend rather than simply replicating the portrait. Such additions may include flags, four small vignettes depicting the apparition sequence, Juan Diego, the Holy Family, various saints, Mary's family tree, angelic musicians, cherubs, clouds, rosaries, religious structures, and garlands of flowers such as lilies and roses.

Guadalupe Today

For nearly five centuries, devotional rituals, festivities, and arts honoring the famous New World Virgin of Guadalupe have gained tremendous popularity. Special masses in her name are celebrated throughout the world on December 12. Celebrants of Guadalupe make pilgrimages—some that last for days and others involving more simple daytime walks. Colorful street processions, virtual pageants of joy, offer buoyant examples of how much she means to her extended family of devotees.

Pilgrimages and Processions

"*¡Viva Guadalupe!*" pilgrims cry as they advance to a shrine, cathedral, or sacred site associated with their shepherdess (*La Pastora*, as some of her Spanish-speaking followers call her). Broiling sun, thick snow, parched deserts, or auto-packed roads do not daunt these dedicated wayfarers. Poverty, age, poor health, and distance do not deter these pilgrims from their overwhelming desire to walk for—and with—La Virgencita. They

A blend of
two female
Mexican
icons—the
Virgin of
Guadalupe
and Frida
Kahlo.

The Arrival, a contemporary painting by Laura Brink.

may complain of sore feet and thirst, but they keep one another company reciting the rosary and singing sacred tunes or *alabados*. Many pilgrims carry a cherished image of her with them during their long journeys. Ladies sport earrings with Guadalupe's face. Hats, belt buckles, T-shirts, scarves, jackets, and other items bearing the Virgin's likeness reflect the pilgrims' bonds with their patroness and their profound trust that her image carries a religious meaning, even protection. Leaders of pilgrimages often wave banners bearing a likeness of La Virgencita above the crowd.

Joy, comfort, and strength of purpose come from the belief that Guadalupe is a fellow pilgrim who walks with them, a member of their communities, a beloved relative at their side. The Virgin is thus not isolated on a lofty canvas or lost in the distant past; she is considered present in these observances. Pilgrimages in the name of Guadalupe are not parades or tours organized by travel agents; they are quests in pursuit of the holy, and they often involve a *manda* or *promesa* (vow or promise). Our Lady of Guadalupe plays a dual role in the pilgrimages that honor her—as a companion pilgrim in time and space and as the transcendent patroness of the journey.

For the past decade, newspapers in Mexico City have reported that three to four million pilgrims flocked to the Basílica de Guadalupe in Mexico City, and the surrounding area known as La Villa de Guadalupe, on Guadalupe's December feast day. Such numbers are reasonable considering that thousands come daily, and each year a total of more than ten million are estimated to find their way to see their "Madre Guadalupe." The faithful, alone or with family and like-minded pilgrims, often end their journeys on their knees, to bow in front of her famous portrait high on the wall above the main altar inside this sacred space. Many making their final approach to the great shrine clutch roses, babies, sleeping bags, canes, or rosaries. Some pilgrims trudge hundreds of miles on foot, often barefoot, while others arrive by subway, bus, bicycle, or automobile. Every day of the year inside the great basilica, prayers and songs are offered to Guadalupe in a variety of languages from the lips of pilgrims who have come from around the world—from the Orient to the Occident, from the Alps to the Andes.

In the great plaza in front of the basilica, families pose for snapshots before stalls hung with likenesses of the tilma portrait (usually enhanced with plastic flowers). Saint Juan Diego is now an important part of these installations as well. Traditional dancers with huge plumed headdresses and sequined costumes weave and sway between these stalls and the standing or kneeling pilgrims. Cameras click, candy bars are devoured, children scoot about teasing one another as jet planes roar overhead. Immediately outside the gates of La Villa, shops and hawkers offer low-budget souvenirs of a visit to the Virgin.

Not all pilgrimages honoring La Morena necessarily fit the Christian tradition of leaving home to visit a hallowed site, saint's tomb, or place of martyrdom. A location with local or general religious meaning frequently serves as a substitute link—such as a rural slope or a patch of ground dedicated to La Madrecita. It is the pilgrims' focus, and their intent, that converts such a site into one with a specific bond to Guadalupe.

Processions honoring Our Lady of Guadalupe are

Young girl in Denver, Colorado.

Stephen Calles and Craig Moya pose with their prize-winning statue at the 2003 Spanish Market, Santa Fe.

A Mexico City pilgrim bears his personal picture of the Virgin on his back.

also time-honored celebrations, although they do not generally include the penance and physical discomforts associated with pilgrimages. They generally take place in a village or urban location within a community and not on remote or harsh land. Faith, tradition, and a sense of *communitas*

are celebrated by the stream of people in processions featuring Guadalupe. An over-flowing sense of joy is the hallmark of these festivities, as seen in the costumes, pageantry, and floats mounted with fantasy tableaux embellished in wild colors.

Modern Portraits

As devotion to Guadalupe and San Juan Diego continues, we see increasing diversity in their visual representations. Artists and artisans depict the Virgin of Guadalupe in two major modes—traditional renderings and more innovative creations. Both genres have been instrumental in perpetuating the Guadalupe story. Often artists confess that their inspiration comes from a transcendent source enhanced by Catholic traditions and the strength of folk devotion. Religious art can never be fully severed from the spiritual concepts of the people who cherish and depict them.

Eventually, artists began to break with tradition by adding visual vignettes of the apparition story to the original portrait and by enhancing its basic format. In the twenty-first century, many artists still illustrate Guadalupe in a traditional, serene style. Such likenesses usually stay close to the basic colors and dress style of Guadalupe as she appeared on the tilma after the alterations at the end of the 1500s. Various added details portray the Virgin as a Christian icon of faith, hope, charity, and spiritual power. Slightly innovative departures from the original tilma image appear in some compositions—such as roses, Juan Diego, or two cherubs tugging at a rosary.

In contrast to the more traditional versions of Guadalupe, we also find new, even startling, creations—some of which shock those bound by strict convictions of what is acceptable in the arts depicting religious persons or events. Bold lines, a kaleidoscope of dazzling colors, and exaggerated facial expressions and poses introduce new pictures of the Virgin to the eyes of the public—however, perhaps this is not so new after all. Old rules and formulas for representing sacred figures in art have been broken again and again over the centuries. The rigid, eyes-ahead Mary stiffly grasping the Christ Child in the art of Byzantium has evolved into Christmas card and calendar illustrations of the Mother of Jesus cuddling her son as they enjoy an exchange of eye contact.

New emblems of Guadalupe are easy to find throughout the Americas on both hand-crafted and machine-made trinkets and souvenirs. These items frequently depart from tradition—for example, the traditional stars on her mantle may now feature designs of chiles, dots, and squiggles, enhanced with glitter, sequins, or buttons.

To countless artisans, both past and present, goes immeasurable credit for expanding the cult of Guadalupe. Her image lives on in the visual arts, so much so that she comes into view at almost every turn, her likeness permanently etched in our memories. By the twentieth century, images of Guadalupe were no longer limited to pious archival service; they became visual adventures. La Madrecita lives in the eyes of her people every day, not just on her feast day.

Her Image Found in Cars, Jewelry, Magnets, and More

Airbrushed images or decals of Guadalupe glow from low-rider automobiles, the "rolling temples" that cruise under her symbolic protection. The driver may wear a belt buckle with a semblance of Guadalupe. Motorcycles, bicycles, and children's tricycles celebrate her on fenders. Gadgets such as gear-shift knobs take Guadalupe inside the cabs of motor vehicles. A plastic replica of Guadalupe may wiggle on a spring glued to a dashboard. Her outline shines from iridescent decals stuck to auto windows,

her image may appear on a vehicle's rear curtains, and medallions with replicas of the Virgin dangle from the rings of ignition keys.

Jewelers celebrate her in earrings, pins, medallions, and buttons. A wee likeness of La Pastora dangling from a leash or collar may protect the family dog. The press of a finger on a spray can with her image can emit a floral scent. People hang ornaments featuring the Virgin on Christmas trees. Ceramic artists immortalize her under permanent glazes in tiles. Guadalupe keeps watch over cyberspace from computer mouse pads. She helps with the task of enlightenment from wall switch plates, long-life candles, night lights, and decorative lamps. Magnets with her image cling to refrigerator doors. The Mother of the People appears on postcards, greeting cards, bookmarks, and in coloring books. She helps believers "keep in touch" with like-minded souls from telephones emblazoned with her image in iridescent colors

Custom
cowboy boots
by Rocket
Buster Boots
of El Paso,
Texas.

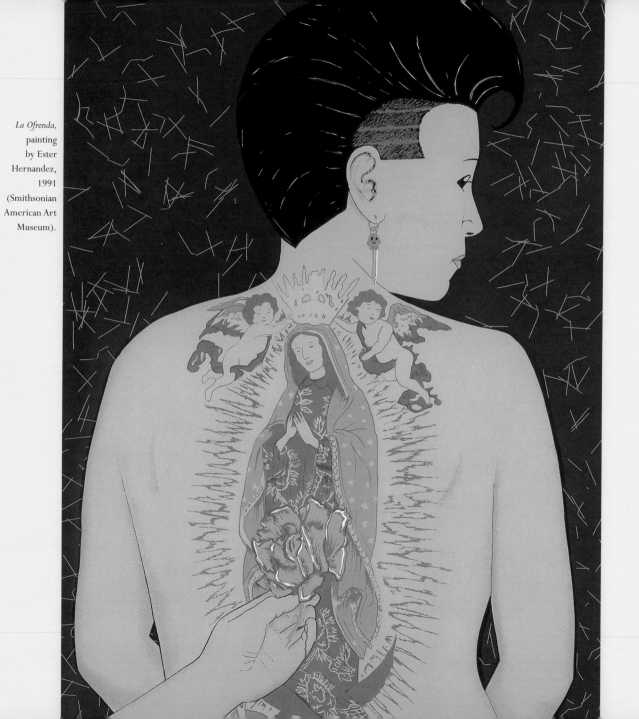

La Ofrenda,
painting
by Ester
Hernandez,
1991
(Smithsonian
American Art
Museum).

Tattoo on
the back of
Santa Fe
boxer
Robbie
Lovato.

Embroidery by Kathleen Sais Lerner, Spanish Market, Santa Fe, New Mexico.

Guadalupe moves the tick and tock of time across the dial faces of watches and clocks.

Architecture provides a vast outlet for celebrating Guadalupe in material and non-material form. Churches large and small, chapels, sanctuaries, and missions, in nearly every style of sacred building, glorify the Virgin of Guadalupe. Private citizens who invite her to be a protectress install free-standing, outdoor shrines on their property to shelter her likeness under brick, mortar, stone, and plastic. These shrines—shelters where whimsy and memory meet—are often bedecked with bits of glitter, buttons, mirror shards, and tiles. Indoors, Guadalupe keeps a silent vigil on home altars where objects, both sacred and personal, may be grouped side by side to bless the household.

Stonemasons may chisel replicas of Guadalupe into sturdy memorials set above graves in cemeteries. Standing between sky and earth, she symbolically bestows eterna

care on the departed as well as on those recently bereaved who have turned to her for solace. Mourners bearing or following a coffin into a church for final rites may wear specially emblazoned T-shirts with a likeness of Guadalupe. These "funeral shirts" also bear the imprint of the dead person's name.

In keeping with the legend of 1531, her followers have no doubt that Guadalupe's involvement with healing endures. Pain-relieving "plasters" with her image offer relief for aches and discomforts. Medallions and other charms with imprints or engravings of Guadalupe are cherished as agents to heal all manner of sicknesses and accidents.

Guadalupe on Cloth

According to the Bible (Acts 19:11–12), God wrought mighty miracles through the hands of Paul, who is credited with curing the sick by touching them with "face cloths or aprons." A link to this biblical legacy can be seen in Guadalupe's portrait on Juan

Diego's cloak, a manifestation of the holy transmitted to cloth. Devotees of the Virgin, especially prisoners, paint likenesses of her on a handkerchief (*paño* in Spanish) to invite her blessings, for they hold that she does not judge their misdeeds. Seamstresses stitch her image glowing with sequins on wearable art, and other needleworkers produce glorious cloth panels of embroidery suited for framing. The Virgin's outline on a bed quilt adds a protective symbol to the warmth of the bedding. Imprints of Guadalupe's face or full body appear in the motifs of machine-manufactured yard goods. Needlecraft skills are put to the special service of adorning clergymen's stoles, and lacemakers transform simple thread into altar cloths and various clerical vestments.

Day-to-day fashion freely borrows Guadalupe's image for T-shirts, the wearable archives of our era. Priests, deacons, mothers, fathers, and children wear them, as well as *peregrinos* and *Guadalupanos* (Spanish words for pilgrims and followers of Guadalupe). We see a quality of "spiritual chic" on jackets brightened with sequins and tunics splashed with her portrait. These articles of clothing do not belittle the Virgin; rather they keep her outwardly close to a wearer who has inward attachment to her. A cap sporting printed or stitched facsimiles of Guadalupe virtually crowns a wearer's head. Tattoos come alive under the skin of the Virgin's devotees as a vision of her is now literally inked into their bodies.

T-shirts with the Virgin's face or full form often carry more than design motifs as they silently broadcast messages such as: LATIN POWER, CRUISIN' TOGETHER, *RAZA UNIDA, POR LA PAZ DEL MUNDO,* and *BARRIO UNIDO.* Others announce that Guadalupe with Pope John Paul II stands for *MEXICO SIEMPRE FIEL.* Since the canonization of San Juan Diego, an influx of new T-shirts has hit Mexico and the U.S. border states, featuring the new saint both alone and with Guadalupe.

Guadalupe, Symbol of the People

Guadalupe has gradually become a dominant symbol of the Mexican people. She evolved from being primarily a religious icon to an agent invoked for public miracles—including victories over plagues and revolutions—and a savior of the disadvantaged. Her role in Mexican life was deeply affected by a neo-Aztec movement that started during the Colonial period of the 1700s and revived in the 1950s and 60s, celebrating classic Mesoamerican culture and its symbols as a wellspring of Mexican identity. The movement was not based on a desire

A mural in San Francisco's Mission District. The nails may refer to the Seven Sorrows of the Blessed Mother.

Doy Gracias de todo Corazón a la S
Virgen de Guadalupe por salvar m
vida en una battalla en contra de
militares de Parral CHIUAHUA.
Venustiano Pereira Enero de 189

A Mexican painting, dated 1897, gives thanks for the
Virgin's protection in battle.

to cut ties to Europe; it was the result of a prolonged identity quest. As the population of her followers included more and more native-born peoples and mestizos, La Morena and La Morenita (The Dark One, The Dear Dark One) joined Guadalupe's list of titles.

Scholars see Nuestra Señora de Guadalupe as the ideal leader of social integration because she steadily evolved to represent the Mexican people themselves. Thus, a once exclusively religious symbol was put to the service of the national honor and social unity, in particular the raising up of the lower classes. The Mexican-born Nobel laureate Octavio Paz wrote of her: "The Virgin is the consolation of the poor, the shield of the weak, the help of the oppressed. In sum, she is the Mother of Orphans."

Guadalupe's devotees place unfailing trust in her, their ultimate mother. They believe that she will always be there to help, cure, and protect them while offering compassion, not condemnation, for their human failings. It is to Guadalupe that her followers address their pleas for intercession. This shepherdess of loving kindness leads them not only across the land in pilgrimages, adding joy to life, but beyond this world into a hoped-for eternal life.

Padre Miguel Hidalgo y Costilla, the Mexican criollo patriot, gave his famous *Grito de Dolores* (the "Cry of Dolores") in the early morning of September 16, 1810. This moving plea was aimed to rouse his fellow Mexicans (Mesoamerican natives, criollos, and mestizos alike) to depose the Spaniards from power and rid the land of foreign control, abusive government, and ruinous taxes. The words of the cry were *"¡Mueran los gachupines! ¡Viva la Virgen de Guadalupe!"* (Death to the Spaniards! Long live the Virgin of Guadalupe!). This famous grito rallied the people to wage the Mexican War of Independence from Spain, which ended in 1821. (A *gachupín* is a derogatory term for a European-born Spaniard living in Mexico, many of whom were hostile to those born in Mexico.)

At the moment the battle cry was uttered, Guadalupe emerged as a symbol of strength and freedom; she stepped beyond the altar forever to be active with her people, the masses. And the people Hidalgo inspired then bestowed upon their nationally rooted Virgin political power as an active maternal force in addition to her role as a gentle manifestation of the biblical Mary.

Padre Hidalgo's troops carried images of Guadalupe with them on poles or reeds, and many wore prints of the Virgin on their hats. In 1859, when the Mexican government under President Benito Juárez divided church and state, the only remaining religious holiday was Guadalupe's feast day,

GUADALUPE AND MORE RECENT CAUSES

Since 1998, an annual torch-relay run called Antorcha Guadalupana—honoring Guadalupe, symbolizing the faith of the Mexican people, and calling for awareness of the rights of Mexican immigrants—has taken place in New York City. In 2002, for the first time, the torch was lit at the Basílica de Guadalupe in Mexico City and then carried more than 3,300 miles to reach New York's Saint Patrick's Cathedral on December 12, passing through forty-five cities along the way, nine in Mexico and thirty-six in the southern and eastern United States.

December 12. Later, Guadalupe's image represented both faith and freedom to the dissidents of the Mexican Revolution, as the troops of Emiliano Zapata and Pancho Villa marched under her flag when they took Mexico City in 1911. Zapata, a Mexican farmer of native blood, became a brilliant leader whose battle cry was for land and liberty for the oppressed. He and his soldiers fought for the return of Indian lands from the central government, carrying banners depicting Guadalupe's image into battle.

In the 1960s and 70s, American-born labor leader César Chávez organized the United Farm Workers movement, in which grape pickers and field workers, many of them migratory Mexican-Americans, successfully demonstrated against unfair labor practices in California. Chávez and his movement's slogan—*Sí se puede* (Yes you can)—are still featured in activist art in a visual cry for justice, and the Virgin of Guadalupe often appeared in the banners,

murals, and posters that promoted his cause. A new fervor in cutting-edge icons springing from these and other movements gives her depictions a potent, symbolic

presence as a modern Christian Virgin who is still invoked and celebrated in the struggles of the oppressed.

Guadalupe adorns one support of an overpass in El Paso, Texas.

Mother of the People

No single factor or event can fully explain the depth and tenacity of faith in the New World's Virgin of Guadalupe. Theology, ethnology, artistry, history, folklore, and the human need to believe that a loving force rules life combine to help explain the enduring veneration of the Mexican Virgin, who eventually became a unique icon.

Guadalupe's prominence comes from her great adaptability and at the same time continuity as a symbol. She has remained steadfastly on the altar and simultaneously has moved beyond it to walk and dance with her people, bury their dead, and name their babies. Much more than just an advocate who takes up the urgent causes of those afflicted in body or mind, the Virgin of Guadalupe is also venerated as a collective mother, compassionate and unfailing, an agent of joy and ease. In Mexico, Guadalupe evolved beyond being solely an agent of miraculous cures and Christian comfort to an icon put to the service of vigorous nationalism and personal liberation.

As she has touched every continent, the "global Guadalupe" has gathered followers of all racial and social categories, especially those for whom she represents the embodiment of the ultimate mother, strong but sensitive to change. She is, indeed, still an icon of the gentle values of the traditional domains of Mary. However, Guadalupe's true power helps her followers cross many borders and barriers: ethnic, geographic, and temporal, along with the imprisonment of personal suffering. Socially oppressed people invoke her, criminals invoke her, feminists invoke her, as do rich and poor alike. Guadalupe thrives and grows in the collective minds and hearts of her devotees; she is the portal, path, or lens through which they can move from the ordinary to the sacred, from the despairs of the day to hope for a promising future, and ultimately from earth to heaven.

East meets West in an international holiday greeting card
by Petra Mathers.

GUADALUPE AND THE AUTHOR

Decades before I was born, my Swiss grandmother made a voyage to Mexico to meet Guadalupe in person. Her notes, scratched in French on weasel-colored vellum, revealed her desire to meet with a Virgin important enough to merit a basilica hung with great chandeliers. Grandmother's epic trip started with an Alpine crossing in a horse-pulled sleigh. She waited in Genoa for a steamship to Gibraltar. From there she sailed to Spain, where she sipped fine sherry before crossing the Atlantic to the Americas. Her notes hinted that she prayed as waves tossed the ship as though it were "a tiny feather in big soup."

Finally she stepped onto the shores of the New World at Vera Cruz. During her Mexican holiday, she bought a small painting of Guadalupe. To make sure the image journeyed safely back to the Alps, she wrapped it in one of her sturdy corsets.

By the time I turned three, my résumé held these facts: I was born Swiss, my Italian father had died before my birth, my mother had no use for a child, and thus I became my grandmother's "sister." One twilight, after a revelation she received in the Alps, Grandmother bundled our belongings, including Guadalupe's portrait, into a huge trunk. We set sail from Venice for Hanoi, in French Indochina, to visit a cousin. There the Mexican painting of Guadalupe hung above my bed, shrouded in netting. For seven more years my grandmother and I shuffled about south Asia. Finally, we fled to the United States to avoid the impending war in Europe. Guadalupe's portrait traveled with us.

When we passed into New York Harbor, via Suez and numerous other ports, a beautiful lady crowned with stars and wearing a long robe greeted us. I asked my grandmother, "Is that our Guadalupe?" She looked at me, patted my head, and said, "Not exactly, but yes, she is a Liberty Lady just like the Virgin Mary of Guadalupe in Mexico."

Even before my birth, it seems, the inscrutable hands of destiny had been at work in my life, and Guadalupe continues to travel with me to this day.

ACKNOWLEDGMENTS

In the course of writing, researching, and doing field work for this book, I benefited from valuable service from many people and institutions. Without their assistance this text would not have been possible.

I wish to express special gratitude to certain libraries and their staffs who offered me extraordinary assistance: the Zimmerman Library at the University of New Mexico, the New York Public Library, the library at the University of Texas at El Paso, the Columbia University Libraries in New York City, the library at the Museo de la Basílica de Guadalupe in Mexico City, and the Biblioteca Nacional in Mexico City.

I am deeply grateful to members of the academic community who generously shared their knowledge with me: Drs. Louise M. Burkhart, G. Benito Cordova, James S. Griffith, Ruth Meredith, Victor Alejandro Sorell, Jeanette Favrot Peterson, and the late Yvonne Lange. Richard Ahlborn of the Smithsonian Institution and Stafford Poole, C.M., set me on the path to productive research.

The list of friends and colleagues who merit special mention include A. Samuel Adelo, the late Anderson Bakewell, S.J., Jenifer Blakemore, José Esquibel, Robin Farwell Gavin, Nancy Hamilton, Nicholas Hererra, Valerie McNown, M.D., "Mr. Milagro," Tey Marianna Nunn, Ana Pacheco, the late Charles W. Polzer, S.J., "Bud" Redding, Father C. Roca, S.F., Susan P. Sullivan, and Landon Young.

There is no praise high enough for Charles Mann, the photographer with the magical eye, who helped bring this book into visual reality.

Charles Mann and I wish to extend our sincere thanks to Rio Nuevo's publishers W. Ross Humphreys and Susan Lowell for their invaluable guidance, and to editor Lisa Cooper for her tireless assistance.

Finally, and always, I thank my children, "Gator" and India, for their unfailing encouragement.

I alone am responsible for the text and any errors.

August 15, 2003
Jacqueline Orsini Dunnington

SELECT BIBLIOGRAPHY

Aguilera, Francisco M., Ernesto Corripio Ahumada, and Guillermo Schulenberg Prado. *Album Conmemorativo del 450 aniversario de las apariciones de Nuestra Señora de Guadalupe.* Mexico City: Ediciones Buena Vista, 1981.

Becerra Tanco, Luis. "Origen milagroso del santuario de Nuestra Señora de Guadalupe." In *Testimonios históricos guadalupanos.* Edited by Ernesto de la Torre Villar and Ramiro Navarro de Anda. Mexico City: Fondo de Cultura Económica, 1982.

Brading, D. A. *Mexican Phoenix: Our Lady of Guadalupe: Image and Tradition across Five Centuries.* Cambridge, England: Cambridge University Press, 2002.

Burckhart, Louise M. *Before Guadalupe: The Virgin Mary in Early Colonial Nahuatl Literature.* IMS Monograph 13. Albany, NY: State University of New York, 2001.

Burrus, Ernest J., S.J. *The Basic Bibliography of the Guadalupan Apparitions (1531–1723).* CARA Studies on Popular Devotion, vol. 4: Guadalupan Studies, no. 5. Washington, D.C.: Center for Applied Research in the Apostolate, 1983.

Callahan, Philip Serna. *The Tilma under Infra-Red Radiation.* CARA Studies on Popular Devotion, vol. 2: Guadalupan Studies, no. 3. Washington, D.C.: Center for Applied Research in the Apostolate, 1981.

Dunnington, Jacqueline Orsini. *Viva Guadalupe!* Photographs by Charles Mann. Santa Fe, NM: Museum of New Mexico Press, 1997.

————. *Guadalupe: Our Lady of New Mexico.* Santa Fe, NM: Museum of New Mexico Press: 1999.

Ferguson, George. *Signs and Symbols in Christian Art.* New York: Oxford University Press, 1959.

Florencia, Francisco de, S.J. *La Estrella del Norte de México.* Madrid: Imprenta de Lorenzo de San Martín, 1785. (An imprint of the original 1688 Mexico City edition.)

Gaspar de Alba, Alicia. *Chicano Art: Inside and Outside the Master's House.* Austin, TX: University of Texas Press, 2000.

Krauze, Enrique. *Mexico: Biography of Power, A History of Modern Mexico 1810–1996.* Translated by Hank Heifetz. New York: HarperCollins Publishers Inc., 1997. (This is my source for the exact wording of the September 16, 1810, *Grito de Dolores*.)

Lafaye, Jacques. *Quetzalcóatl and Guadalupe: The Formation of Mexican National Consciousness 1531–1813.* Translated by Benjamin Keen. Chicago: University of Chicago Press, 1976.

Lasso [Laso, Lazo] de la Vega, Luis. *Huey tlamahuiçoltica omonexiti ilhuicac tlatocihuapilli Santa María totlaçonantzin Guadalupe in nican huey altepenahuac Mexico itocayocan Tepeyacac.* Mexico City: Imprenta de Juan Ruiz, 1649. (Written in Nahuatl, this text is known today as the *Nican Mopohua*.)

Leatham-Smith, Miguel. "Indigenista Hermaneutics." *Folklore Forum* 22:1–2 (1989). (My source for the theory that Guadalupe's Nahuatl name was Tlecuauhtlapcupeuh.)

Lee, Fr. George, C.S.Sp. *Our Lady of Guadalupe, Patroness of the Americas.* New York: Catholic Book Publishing Co, 1897, reprinted 1947.

Paz, Octavio. *The Labyrinth of Solitude: Life and Thought in Mexico.* Translated by Lysander Kemp. New York: Grove Press, 1961.

Peterson, Jeanette Favrot. "The Virgin of Guadalupe: Symbol of Conquest or Liberation?" *Art Journal* 51, no. 4 (Winter 1992).

Poole, Stafford, C.M. *Our Lady of Guadalupe: The Origins and Sources of a Mexican National Symbol, 1531–1797.* Tucson, AZ: University of Arizona Press, 1995. (This source offers the most recent scholarly translation of Juan Diego's story to date.)

Rodriguez, Jeanette. *Our Lady of Guadalupe: Faith and Empowerment among Mexican American Women.* Austin: University of Texas Press, 1994.

Sahagún, Bernardino de. *Conquest of New Spain: 1585.* Revision. Translated and edited by Howard F. Cline, with introduction and notes by S. L. Cline. Salt Lake City: University of Utah Press, 1989.

Sánchez, Miguel. *Imagen de la virgen María, Madre de Dios Guadalupe.* México: Imprenta de la Viuda de Bernardo Calderón, 1648. (This account, written in Spanish, offers the earliest-known major written account of the apparition of Our Lady to Juan Diego.)

The Story of Guadalupe: Luis Laso de la Vega's Huei Tlamalhuiçoltica of 1649. Edited and translated by Lisa Sousa, Stafford Poole, C.M., and James Lockhart. UCLA Latin American Studies Volume 84: UCLA Latin American Center Publications. Stanford, CA: Stanford University Press, 1998. (The quotes from the 1531 apparition sequence come from this text.)

Stratton, Suzanne L. *The Immaculate Conception in Spanish Art.* Cambridge, England: Cambridge University Press, 1994.

Teresa de Mier, Fray Servando. *The Memoirs of Fray Servando de Mier.* Translated by Helen Lane. Edited and introduced by Susana Rotker. New York: Oxford University Press, 1998.

Wroth, William. *Christian Images in Hispanic New Mexico.* Colorado Springs, CO: The Taylor Museum of the Colorado Springs Fine Arts Center, 1982.